USE YOUR BRAIN

USE YOUR BRAIN

BY PAUL SHOWERS   Illustrated by Rosalind Fry

THOMAS Y. CROWELL COMPANY   NEW YORK

LET'S-READ-AND-FIND-OUT SCIENCE BOOKS

Editors: *DR. ROMA GANS*, Professor Emeritus of Childhood Education, Teachers College, Columbia University

DR. FRANKLYN M. BRANLEY, Chairman and Astronomer of The American Museum–Hayden Planetarium

L.C. Card 79-157646

ISBN 0-690-85410-2
    0-690-85411-0 (LB)

1   2   3   4   5   6   7   8   9   10

USE YOUR BRAIN

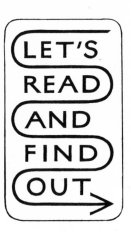

Knock on your head with your knuckles.
Knock on top. Knock above your ears. Knock your
   forehead.
Can you hear the hollow sound?
The top part of your head is hollow inside—like a
   pumpkin.
It is hollow but it is not empty.
Your brain is in the hollow part.

Your brain is what you think with. It is soft and
  gray and wrinkled.
It is made up of millions and millions of tiny parts
  called cells. They are all jammed together.
The cells are tied to one another by millions and
  millions of tiny, thin threads.
These threads are called nerves.

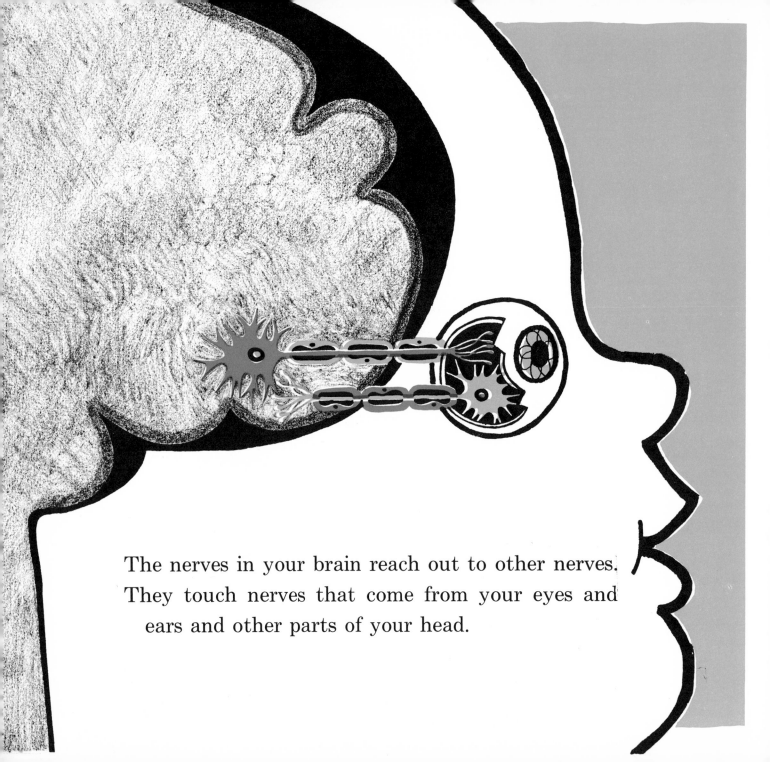

The nerves in your brain reach out to other nerves.
They touch nerves that come from your eyes and
ears and other parts of your head.

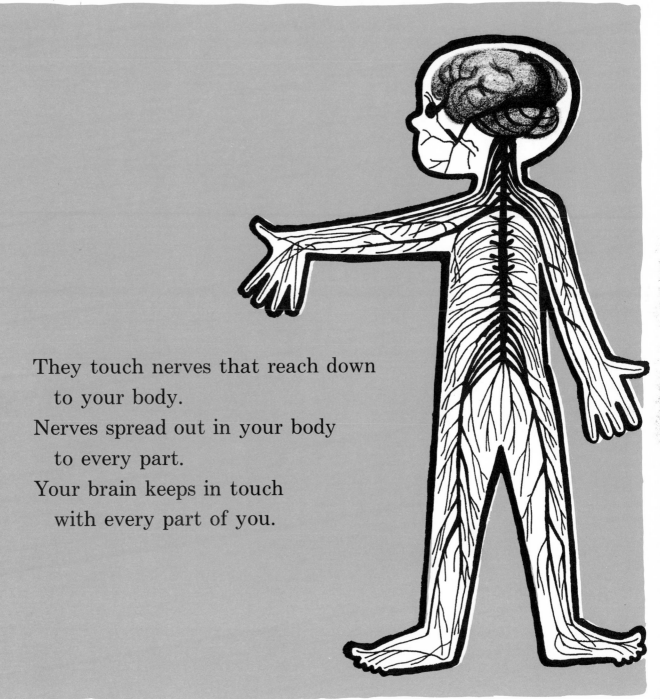

They touch nerves that reach down
   to your body.
Nerves spread out in your body
   to every part.
Your brain keeps in touch
   with every part of you.

5

The nerves are like little telephone wires.
They carry messages to your brain.
This is how it happens.
The sun shines in the window. Light comes into your
  eye.
The nerves of your eye send messages to your brain.
You know it is morning and time to get up.

A fire truck sounds its siren. The noise comes into your ear.
The nerves of your ear send messages to your brain.
You know a fire truck is passing by outside.

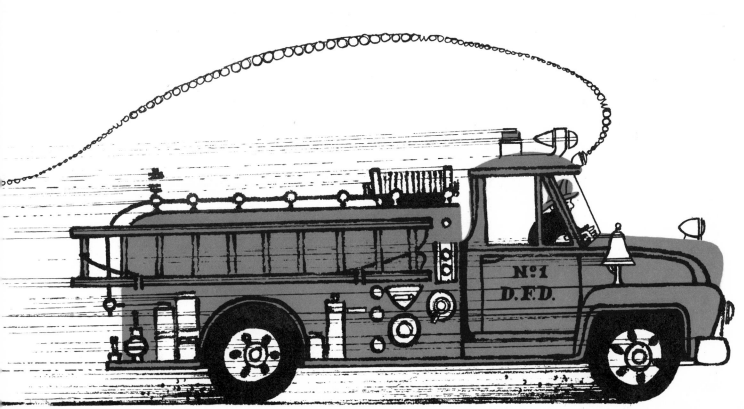

Nerves carry messages to your brain from every part
of your body:
from your legs and your ears,
from your tongue and your nose,
from your stomach and eyes and the palms of your
hands,
from your arms and your teeth and your toes.

You don't have nerves in your fingernails or your
   hair.
That's why it doesn't hurt when you cut them.
They have no nerves to send messages to your brain.

Nerves carry messages also from your brain out to
    your body.
Suppose you think you are going to miss the bus.
You know you must hurry.
Your brain sends a message to your legs—and you
    start running.

When you are ready to turn this page, your brain
   will send a message to your hand and to your arm.
It will work quicker than a wink.
You won't even notice.
You will simply decide to turn this page—and you
   will turn it.

ABcdefGHifme

WV

Xa y U

yn T

mZ is

jklMnOpqRs

Your brain does many things.
You use your brain to remember.
You remember the alphabet
and your best friend's face
and the taste of ice cream
with your brain.

Your brain helps you learn to do things.
It helps you learn to skip and turn cartwheels—to
ride a bicycle and dive.

You are learning to read the words
on this page with your brain.

Someday your brain may help you learn to
play a guitar
or drive a car
or fly a jet.

Your brain is very important. It is carefully protected
from harm.
It has thick, hard bone all around it, called the skull.
Your brain floats in a fluid in the hollow part of
your head.
The fluid is like a cushion.
It keeps your brain from being bumped when you
turn a somersault.

You need to take care of your brain.
Most of the time it does its work very well.
It takes in messages quick as a flash.
It sends out messages just as fast.
Then you feel fine. Everything goes just right.

21

But sometimes your brain doesn't work so well.
When it is tired, it slows down.
It gets its messages mixed up.
Then things go wrong for you.
You forget. You make mistakes. You can't pay
attention—even to TV.

When your brain is tired you get sleepy.
Your brain is telling you it wants a rest.
It is time for you to take your brain to bed.

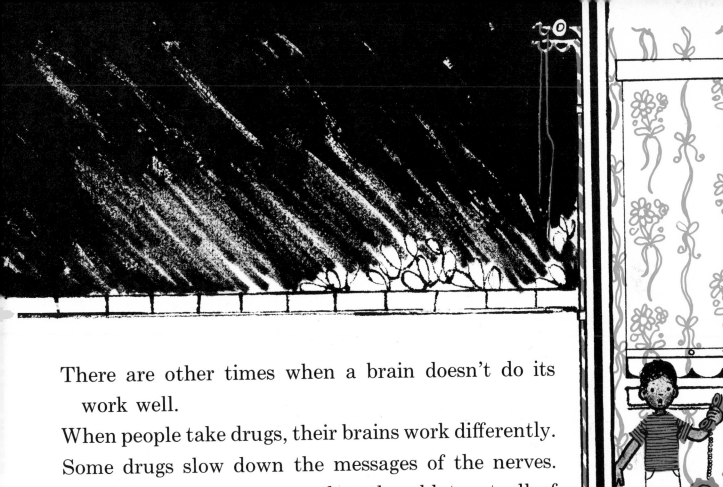

There are other times when a brain doesn't do its
work well.

When people take drugs, their brains work differently.

Some drugs slow down the messages of the nerves.

Some drugs are so strong that they blot out all of
the messages.

Strong drugs are like a storm that tears down all
the telephone wires.

Then none of the messages can get through.

Alcohol is a drug. It is in whiskey and beer.

When a man drinks too much beer or whiskey, he gets drunk.

The messages between his brain and his body are all mixed up.

He can't walk straight. He may fall down.

If he drives a car, he steers badly.

He may go too fast. He can have a bad accident.

There are other bad drugs, too.
They can do even worse things to your brain than
    alcohol.

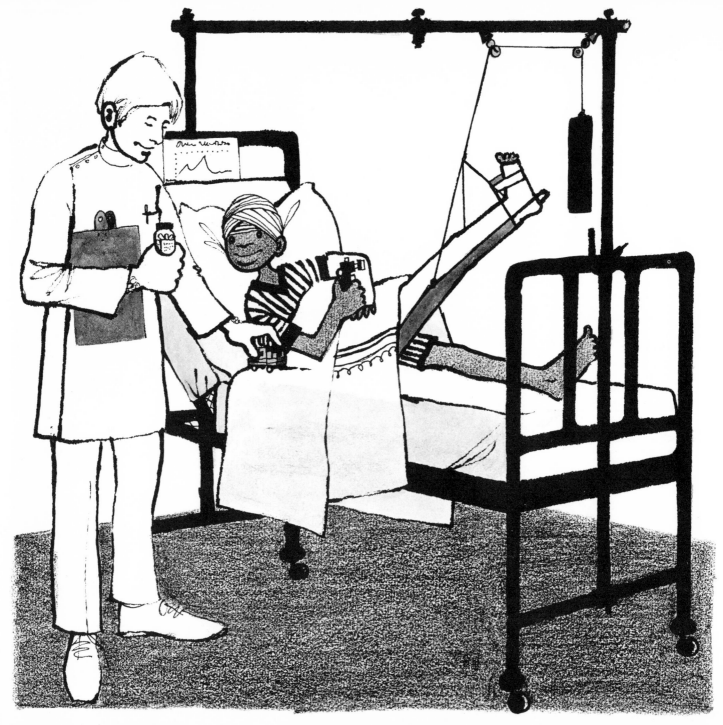

But not all drugs are bad.

There are many kinds. Some of them are good.

They are used in medicines to help people when they
   are sick.

Doctors tell us when to take them.

If you didn't have a brain, you couldn't do any-thing.

You wouldn't know anything.

You might live and grow—like a cabbage or a tomato.

But you wouldn't know any more than a tomato knows.

And a tomato doesn't know anything.

It doesn't even know it's a tomato.

33

ABOUT THE AUTHOR

Paul Showers is a New York newspaperman and writer of more than a dozen books for children. He first became interested in making books for young readers after watching his own children struggle with the "See, Sally, see" books of the 1950's ("television's greatest boon," he calls them). His own books, most of them in the Lets-Read-and-Find-Out series, have thoroughly proved that children's books can be both lively and worth while.

Mr. Showers began newspaper work on the Detroit *Free Press*. Then came the New York *Herald Tribune*, a brief stint on the New York *Sunday Mirror* and, for the past twenty-five years, the Sunday *New York Times*. Mr. Showers was born in Sunnyside, Washington, and has an A.B. degree from the University of Michigan.

ABOUT THE ILLUSTRATOR

Rosalind Fry has lived in and traveled through most of her native Australia. Born in Brisbane, Queensland, she lived on a farm in Armidale, and then during World War II, journeyed 2,500 miles across the desert to Perth in Western Australia. She later moved to Melbourne and now lives in Sydney with her husband and five children.

A recipient of a diploma of illustration from Australia's National Art School, Miss Fry is a well-known illustrator. Her pictures have appeared in several books published both in the United States and abroad.

DATE DUE